SPOTLIGHT ON AMERICAN HISTORY

The War of 1812
New Challenges for a New Nation

Pilar Alvarez

PowerKiDS press™

NEW YORK

Published in 2017 by The Rosen Publishing Group, Inc.
29 East 21st Street, New York, NY 10010

Book Design: Tanya Dellaccio

Photo Credits: Cover, p. 17 Universal History Archive / Universal Images Group/Getty Images; p. 5 DEA PICTURE LIBRARY/De Agostini Picture Library/Getty Images; p. 6 Georgios Kollidas/Shutterstock.com; p. 7 De Agostini / A. Dagli Orti/De Agostini Picture Library/Getty Images; p. 9 Print Collector / Hulton Fine Art Collection/Getty Images; pp. 10, 11, 13, 19 courtesy of Library Of Congress; p. 12 https://commons.wikimedia.org/wiki/File:Rembrandt_Peale_-_William_Henry_Harrison_-_Google_Art_Project.jpg; p. 14 https://commons.wikimedia.org/wiki/File:1812_War_Declaration.jpg; p. 15 https://commons.wikimedia.org/wiki/File:James_Madison.jpg; pp. 18, 21 Everett Historical/Shutterstock.com p. 20 https://commons.wikimedia.org/wiki/File:Andrew_Jackson.jpg.

Library of Congress Cataloging-in-Publication Data

Names: Alvarez, Pilar F., 1986- author.
Title: The War of 1812 : new challenges for a new nation / Pilar Alvarez.
Description: New York : PowerKids Press, 2016. | Series: Spotlight on
  American history | Includes index.
Identifiers: LCCN 2015049084 | ISBN 9781508149613 (pbk.) | ISBN 9781508149477 (library bound) | ISBN 9781508149255 (6 pack)
Subjects: LCSH: United States--History--War of 1812--Juvenile literature.
Classification: LCC E354 .A48 2016 | DDC 973.5/2--dc23
LC record available at http://lccn.loc.gov/2015049084

Manufactured in the United States of America

CPSIA Compliance Information: Batch #BS16PK: For further information contact Rosen Publishing, New York, New York at 1-800-237-9932.

CONTENTS

PRESERVING A NATION

The United States officially became its own country in 1783, after eight years of fighting for independence during the American Revolution. In the years that followed, the United States doubled in size through the Louisiana Purchase. Americans started moving west of the Appalachian Mountains. The country was changing, gaining an **identity**, and growing stronger.

People of the new nation may not have expected war to return to their soil so soon after it had ended. But in 1812, the United States announced it was once again at war with Great Britain.

The War of 1812 is, at times, hard to understand. The war had **complicated** causes that began years before fighting broke out. Its outcome wasn't exactly clear. However, the War of 1812 helped other nations see the United States as a strong country. And it showed the world that Americans were ready to fight to protect and preserve their growing nation.

During the War of 1812, battles took place throughout the United States, from New York State in the North to New Orleans in the South. The Battle of Plattsburgh in New York is shown here.

BACKGROUND TO WAR

The War of 1812 was caused by conflicts that happened in Europe in the early 19th century. Napoleon Bonaparte became the leader of France in 1799. In 1804, he declared himself emperor. Under Napoleon, France gained control of much of Europe through the Napoleonic Wars. Great Britain and France were at war during this time.

The United States stayed neutral during these wars.

Napoleon Bonaparte

Napoleon and his army invaded Russia in 1812. The invasion failed terribly and began weakening Napoleon's leadership in France.

This means it didn't take sides. Neutrality presented a great trade opportunity. France and Britain weren't trading with each other because they were at war. The United States wasn't at war, so American merchants could trade with both countries. When U.S. merchants or businesses sent ships to Britain and France, they expected their ships to travel freely.

At this time, the United States believed in the idea that "free ships make free goods." This means countries couldn't **interfere** with ships that carried goods to or from their enemies. In other words, the goods were considered "free" when they were on a neutral country's ship.

CAUGHT IN THE MIDDLE

Even though the United States wanted to trade with both countries, both France and Britain tried to keep it from happening. In 1805, the British tried to **blockade** French ports. France responded by cutting off Britain's access to trade ships. This went a step further in 1806, when France said it would view ships that visited British ports as enemies. A later law said France had the right to capture ships that had passed through British ports.

In response, Britain passed the Orders in Council on November 11, 1807. This order said that neutral ships had to get a special license from the British before they could trade with France or colonies owned by France. American merchant ships were stuck in the middle. They risked capture by the French or punishment by the British Royal Navy. It was a dangerous time to be on a merchant ship, but there were many opportunities to make money.

Sailing across the ocean on huge ships, American merchants brought goods from Britain or France back to the United States. They could then trade the "American" goods to other countries.

THE U.S. RESPONDS

Americans were angry that Britain **violated** their trading rights. They became even angrier when Britain stopped American ships, took the sailors off them, and forced the men to become part of the British Royal Navy. This practice was called impressment. Many of the seamen who were impressed were British citizens or subjects who worked on American ships. American seamen were impressed, too. By 1811, at least 6,000 people who claimed to be American citizens were forced to join the British navy.

To many Americans, impressment went against the right to freedom—an idea the United States was built on.

In this political cartoon from 1808, Thomas Jefferson defends the Embargo Act to angry American merchants who were losing money. Jefferson argues the policy will gain Napoleon's protection and favor. Napoleon stands behind Jefferson, encouraging him to defend the act.

The United States responded to these issues by passing the Embargo Act in 1807. Passed under President Thomas Jefferson, the Embargo Act **prohibited** trade with all European nations. It also banned the importation, or bringing in, of British goods.

The Embargo Act actually hurt the United States economy. The Non-Intercourse Act replaced it in 1809. This act prohibited trade with just France and Britain, but said trade could start again if those countries changed their policies. Neither country paid attention, and the **chaos** continued.

UNFRIENDLY RELATIONS

Back on American soil, issues at home also led to war. During this time, many Americans believed it was the United States' duty to occupy land from coast to coast. Americans began moving west and settling on land that belonged to Native American peoples.

Relations between Native Americans and settlers weren't always friendly. Two Shawnee men, Tecumseh and Tenskwatawa, formed a

William Henry Harrison led forces that defeated the Native American forces during the Battle of Tippecanoe. Harrison became a hero of the War of 1812 and, later, president of the United States.

U.S. forces lost 62 men in the Battle of Tippecanoe. It is unknown how many Native American lives were lost.

confederation to fight the growing American presence in their territory. They lived in present-day Indiana.

Britain controlled Canada at this time, so its presence in North America was strong. Some Americans felt the British made relations between them and native peoples worse. Many Native Americans **allied** with the British after U.S. forces defeated the Indian confederacy during the Battle of Tippecanoe in 1811.

Some people suspected the British were supplying Native Americans with weapons to attack Americans. To be free of this threat, Americans felt they had to get the British out of Canada. War was quickly approaching.

MR. MADISON'S WAR

In 1811, President James Madison called a meeting of Congress. A group of congressmen called the War Hawks spoke out about Britain and its policies. Led by Henry Clay, a congressman from Kentucky, the War Hawks complained about the Orders in Council policy. They spoke against impressment, and shared concern over Britain's relationship with Native American groups. The War Hawks pressed for war, and their argument was convincing. On June 18, 1812,

TWELFTH CONGRESS OF THE UNITED STATES;

At the First Session.

Begun and held at the city of Washington, in the territory of Columbia, on Monday the fourth day of November, one thousand eight hundred and eleven.

AN ACT *declaring war between the United Kingdom of Great Britain and Ireland and the dependencies thereof, and the United States of America and their territories.*

Be it enacted by the Senate and House of Representatives of the United States of America in Congress assembled, That

declaration of war against Great Britain

Mainland Britain was thousands of miles away across the Atlantic Ocean. Attacking Canada was the fastest way to reach the British.

The War of 1812 is often called "Mr. Madison's War," since it began while he was in office.

Madison signed a declaration of war against Great Britain.

Britain wasn't interested in going to war with the United States. It was more focused on its troubles with France. Yet Britain needed to protect its claims in Canada. With few soldiers to spare, the Canadian **militia** and Native Americans helped defend the border.

In July 1812, U.S. forces tried to invade Canada. However, the U.S. military was weak and retreated quickly without firing any shots. In August, Britain captured Detroit in present-day Michigan. Other U.S. attempts to take Canadian land failed miserably. This greatly hurt American **morale**.

BATTLES AT SEA

The British military outnumbered the U.S. military, both in soldiers and equipment. However, the U.S. Navy won important victories in the early months of the war.

The USS *Constitution* was a large warship. In 1812, it left Boston to meet the HMS *Guerriere* near Halifax, which is in Canada. The ships fired cannons at each other for at least three hours. The *Guerriere* was so damaged that the *Constitution*'s captain, Isaac Hull, burned it rather than claiming it as a prize. This was the first major victory over the British. After this battle, the USS *Constitution* was nicknamed "Old Ironsides."

On September 10, 1813, an American lookout spotted British ships approaching American forces on Lake Erie. Though the British were successful at first, Master Commandant Oliver Hazard Perry's skillful command of his **fleet** helped the United States win the battle. This victory allowed the United States to control Lake Erie for the rest of the war, and it cut off Britain's supply routes to Detroit. Eventually, the British abandoned the city.

Commander Perry is known for the message on his personal battle flag: "Don't give up the ship."

BURNING THE CAPITAL

Some historians say the United States might have been more successful in the beginning of the war since Britain was more focused on its problems with France. When those problems ended in 1814, Britain could focus on its war with the United States.

Britain's strategy involved **raiding** and burning villages along the East Coast. In August 1814, about 4,000 British troops arrived in the Chesapeake Bay region. They traveled down the Patuxent River, landing in Maryland. They were headed for Washington, D.C.

the burning of Washington, D.C.

The events at Fort McHenry inspired a very famous song. Francis Scott Key was aboard a ship in Baltimore Harbor when the British bombed Fort McHenry. The next morning, he saw the United States flag flying high over the fort. He wrote a poem called "Defense of Fort M'Henry," which later became "The Star Spangled Banner." It has been the U.S. national anthem since 1931.

President Madison had gotten word that British forces planned to attack the capital, but little was done to protect it. People began fleeing the city as the troops advanced. On August 24, the British marched into the city and burned the White House, the Capitol building, and more. They then moved to Baltimore, Maryland. There, American forces fought the British. Warships **bombarded** Fort McHenry, but they failed to defeat it. The British retreated soon after.

JACKSON AND NEW ORLEANS

The United States and Britain entered peace discussions in 1814. On December 24, 1814, they signed the Treaty of Ghent, which officially ended the war. The news took months to reach the United States, where fighting continued.

Andrew Jackson from Tennessee led American forces against the Creek Indians from 1813 to 1814. Allied with the British, the

Andrew Jackson

Andrew Jackson leads his troops during the Battle of New Orleans.

Creeks had raided settlements in the American South. Jackson's troops crushed the Creeks, and Jackson became a major general in the U.S. Army.

In late 1814, Jackson learned that British troops planned to capture the city of New Orleans. Jackson arrived ahead of them and assembled a rather unusual army. Made of militiamen, free black men, Native Americans, and even pirates, the army was unskilled and outnumbered by the British. However, it won the Battle of New Orleans on January 8 after hours of fighting. Jackson became a national hero.

THE WAR ENDS

Congress approved the Treaty of Ghent on February 16, 1815. President Madison signed it, and the war was officially over. News was slow to reach the South and places on the American frontier, so fighting continued for a few months after the treaty was signed.

The War of 1812 didn't really have a clear outcome. Neither side could claim it had won. The United States didn't cause Britain to change the trade or impressment policies that began the war. Boundaries between British territory and American territory stayed the same. So why is this war important?

The War of 1812 helped the United States gain an identity. Americans felt proud that their army and navy were able to defeat Britain's strong military in some battles. The events of the war inspired a patriotic song that later became our national anthem. Two of the war's heroes, Andrew Jackson and William Henry Harrison, later became president. While the War of 1812 may not be memorable to some, the new nation skillfully faced its challenges and became stronger for it.

GLOSSARY

allied (AA-lyd): Joined in support of a cause.

blockade (blah-KAYD): A way of sealing off a place to prevent goods or people from entering or leaving.

bombard (bahm-BARD): To attack continuously.

chaos (KAY-ahs): Complete confusion.

complicated (KAHM-pluh-kay-tihd): Hard to understand.

confederation (kuhn-feh-duh-RAY-shun): A group of people united for a certain cause.

fleet (FLEET): A group of ships.

identity (eye-DEHN-tuh-tee): Who or what something is.

interfere (ihn-tuhr-FEER): To keep something from being carried out properly.

militia (muh-LIH-shuh): A civilian military force.

morale (muh-RAL): Confidence or excitement over something.

prohibit (proh-HIH-but): To refuse to allow.

raid (RAYD): To suddenly attack by surprise.

violate (VY-uh-layt): To break or not respect a rule.

INDEX

PRIMARY SOURCE LIST

Page 11: Political cartoon about the Embargo Act. Created by Cruikshank. Published by Walker & Cornhill. Hand-colored etching. October 15, 1808. Now kept in the Library of Congress Prints and Photographs Division, Washington, D.C.

Page 12: Portrait of William Henry Harrison. Created by Rembrandt Peale. Oil on canvas. ca. 1813. Now kept at the National Portrait Gallery at the Smithsonian Institution, Washington, D.C.

Page 15: Portrait of James Madison. Created by John Vanderlyn. Oil on canvas. 1816. Now kept at the White House, Washington, D.C.

WEBSITES

Due to the changing nature of Internet links, PowerKids Press has developed an online list of websites related to the subject of this book. This site is updated regularly. Please use this link to access the list: www.powerkidslinks.com/soah/1812